Want to draw the most famous anime characters?

Email us at

yukiyoung.art@gmail.com

Please use the title "How To Draw Famous Anime Characters" in your email and we will send a free step-by-step tutorial that helps you draw the famous anime characters **in Chibi style** effortlessly!

TABLE OF CONTENT

SHADOW & HIGHLIGHT   135

PRACTICE   136

//////////// : Fundamental Content

FUNDAMENTAL OF CHIBI

What is Chibi?

In Japanese, Chibi is a slang standing for "small" or "short", and this word is often used in the context of kawaii and cuteness. Interestingly, Chibi is a chibi version of the word chibiru (禿ちびる) - which means "tiny, rounded thing" in the motherland of manga and anime.

For anime and manga fans, the word Chibi immediately reminds them of characters who have big heads and small bodies, with giant round cute eyes. This style is also known as "Super Deformed" (SD), and often has a head to body ratio between 1:1 and 1:2. Chibi character's facial features are often gathered toward the center of the face.

The first waves of Chibi were introduced to the West through anime. One of the most noticeable anime is the Sailor Moon - which is believed as the first one that brings chibi to the West - in the name of Sailor Chibimoon.

It's extremely rare to use chibi style for a whole anime series, but the use of chibi in anime and manga is quite popular. Most of the time, it appears for the purp -ose of depicting scenes that are funny, cute, and humorous. Moreover, anime and manga fans believe that the easiest way to draw their beloved character is using chibi style.

An example of chibi character

Basic Drawing Materials

Drawing is one of the most popular hobbies in the world; gives us the joy and the feeling of being rewarded by encouraging us on using our imagina -tion, hand skills, and the sense of flow. Whenever we want, and wherever we like to draw, we can do it immediately.

To draw anime and manga character in Chibi style, we should prepare a little more basic materials:

Pencils: a collection of different pencils (2B, 6B, HB, and so on) give us more options on sketching & drawing the cha -racters. Having more pencils also benefit us to concentrate on drawing without worrying about any issues that can happen to a pencil and interrupt our flow of drawing.

Brushed pen: use it when you're happy with the pencil sketching - to make your art the final one on the paper.

Eraser: a great tool to remove the con -tainers/the initial sketch lines of the drawing. It's also used for making us being very confident in drawing, with its slogan "Mistakes with pencils? I am here to fix them all". Sometimes, using an eraser as a special brush could make the drawing more interesting.

Ruler: Dividing the character's con -tainer by a specific ratio (which is mentioned on page 9) with a ruler will save you a lot of time.

Chibi Character's Ratio

●●The Ratio Overview

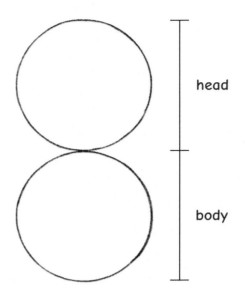

head

body

Notice that the size of the head & the body is the same.

Use two similar circles to sketch the head and the body part.

●● Head Ratio

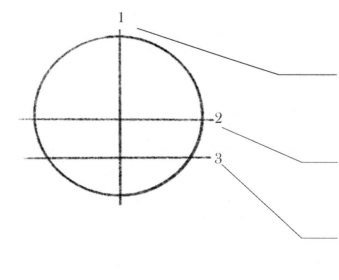

Draw a circle.

Divide the circle into two equal parts horizontally, using no.1 line.

Using no.2 line to divide the circle into two equal parts vertically.

Divide the bottom half of the circle into two equal parts vertically again, using no.3 line.

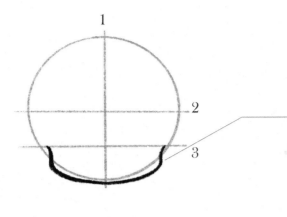

First, draw the cheek from the no.3 line

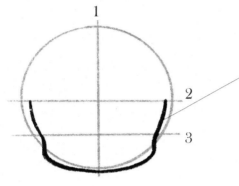

After that, draw the temples.

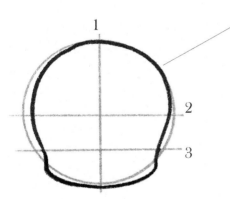

Finally, draw the forehead.

Proportion Of A Face

Eyes

The eyes' height is equal to the distance
between 1st line and 2nd line, meanwhile
the eyes' width is equal to $\frac{1}{5}$ of the
face's width.

Notice

The distance between
the eyes is equal to $\frac{1}{5}$
of the face width, too.

Ear:

Draw the ear on
2nd line.

Mouth & Nose:

Draw the mouth and nose like above.

Notice that they are on the vertical line.

••• Proportion Of A Body

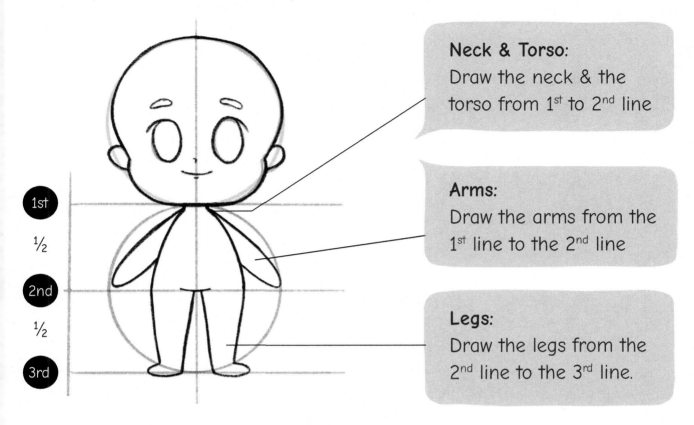

Neck & Torso:
Draw the neck & the torso from 1st to 2nd line

Arms:
Draw the arms from the 1st line to the 2nd line

Legs:
Draw the legs from the 2nd line to the 3rd line.

➡ Wrap Up: Ratio Of The Face & The Body

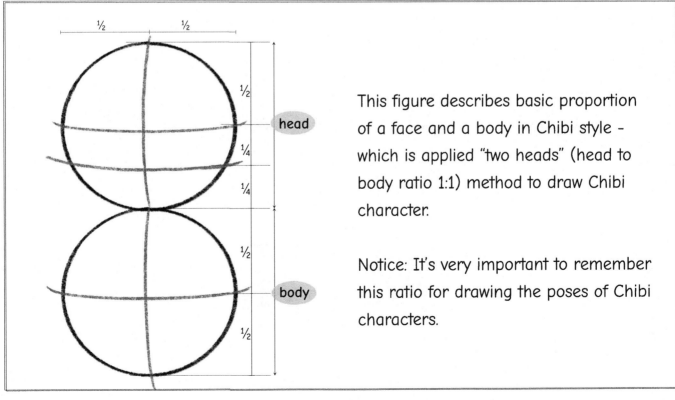

This figure describes basic proportion of a face and a body in Chibi style - which is applied "two heads" (head to body ratio 1:1) method to draw Chibi character.

Notice: It's very important to remember this ratio for drawing the poses of Chibi characters.

DETAILS

Eyes

The eyes of Chibi characters are way easier compared to the eyes of manga characters. This step-by-step drawing tutorial below is a primary way of drawing **basic Chibi eyes** and it can be used in almost all cases.

Step 1: Draw 02 oval shapes equally

Step 2: Draw the pea's shape as above. The pea's size is around ½ of the eye.

Step 3: Draw a small circle at the left corner of the eye

Step 4: Draw a smaller one above the right side of the pea.

Step 5: Colorize all the other areas of the eyes using black color

Step 6: Draw an arc line above the eyes to create the eyelid.

Step 7: Draw the eyelashes. Done!

Extension: Some Other Eyes Style To Draw

Note: Change the pupil's position (the white circle dot) will make the different views of the eyes.

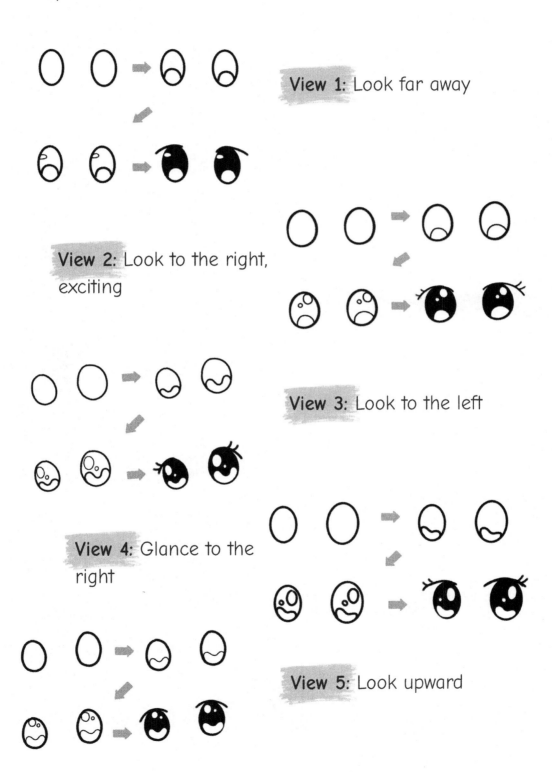

View 1: Look far away

View 2: Look to the right, exciting

View 3: Look to the left

View 4: Glance to the right

View 5: Look upward

Note: The boy's eyes in chibi are often in the square or rectangle shapes

View 6: Glance to the left

View 7: Being nostalgic

View 8: Being adorable

Nose & Mouth

It's necessary to draw the mouth and nose as simple as you can.

Nose:

It's normal not to draw or just draw in very small style like this

Mouth:

Just draw simply like the shapes below

Some mouth styles using for describing certain facial expressions:

⌣̄   : normal

⌣   : slightly smile

⌢   : unhappy / boring

◯   : confused

⌃   : angry

⬭   : scared

⊙   : taunting

◯   : surprising

▽   : happy/excited

Ears

Simply draw like this

Eyebrows

Draw them with small and short lines to make them more adorable

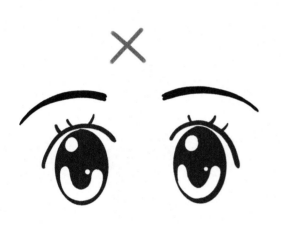

DON'T: draw them with long, complicated lines.

DO: draw them short and simple.

Emotions

It's essential to express successfully the emotions and soul of Chibi characters. This sounds complicated, but actually, with this formula, you can describe all the emotions at the primary level:

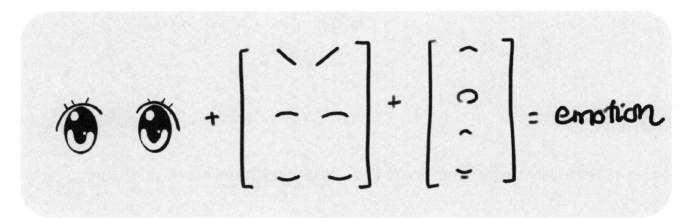

Basic Eyes + Different Eyebrows Direction + Different Mouth Styles = Different Emotions.

Examples

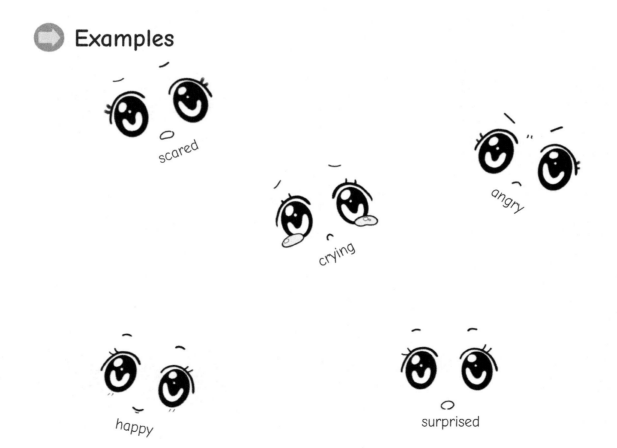

scared

crying

angry

happy

surprised

16

 # Crying

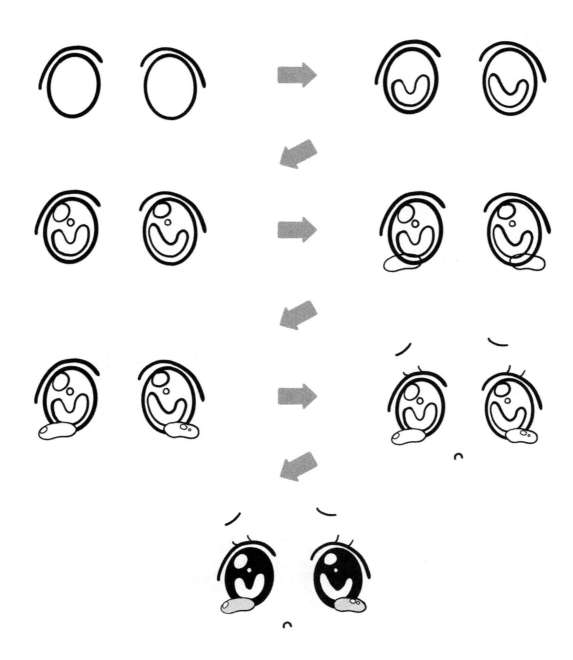

Angry

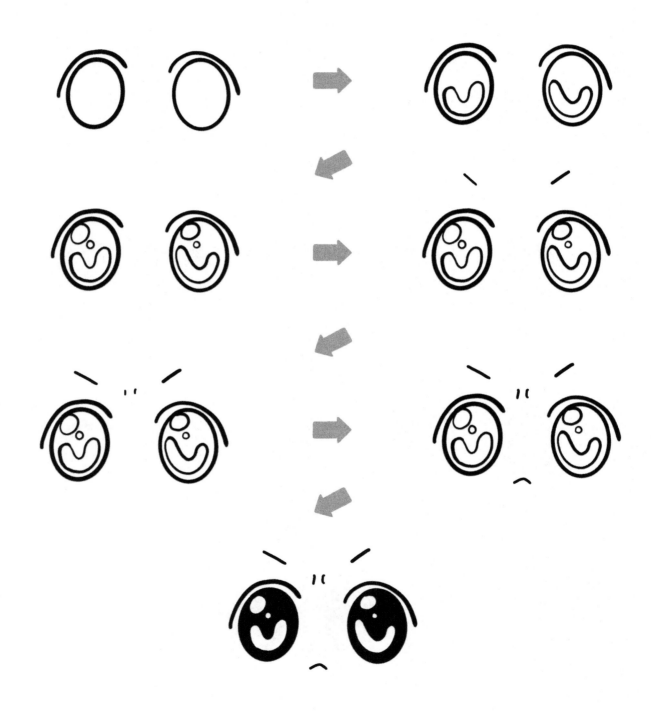

Surprised

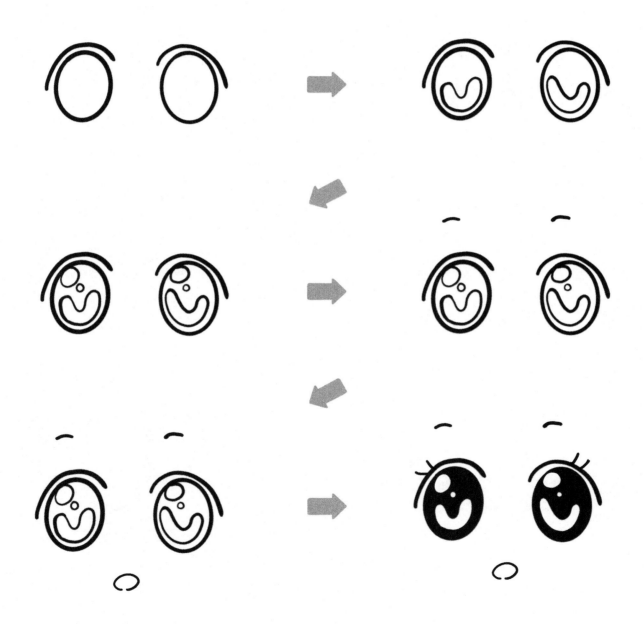

Happy

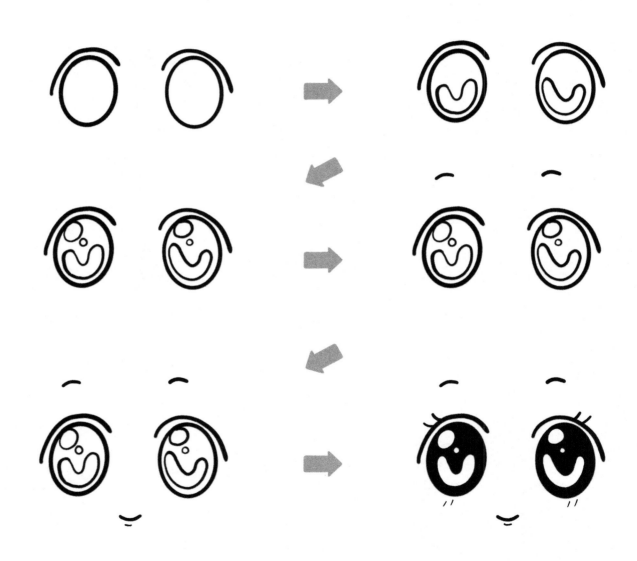

Sleepy

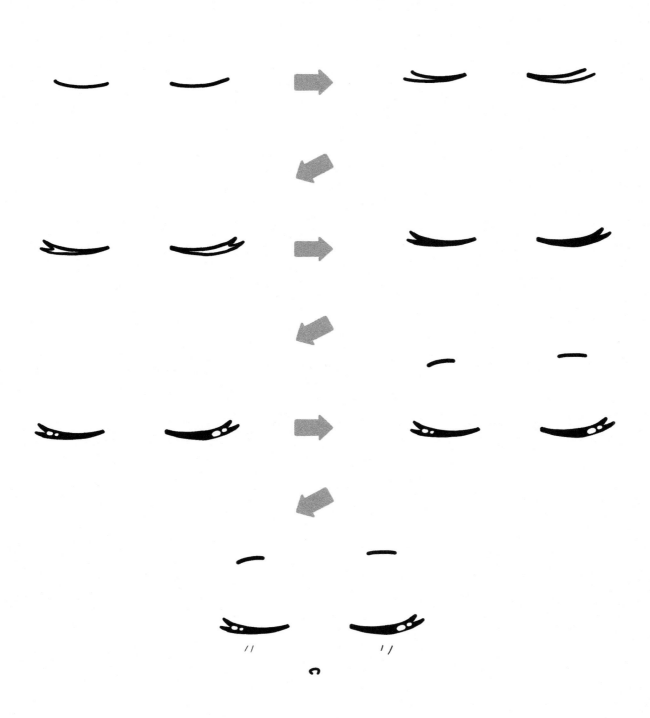

Embarrassed

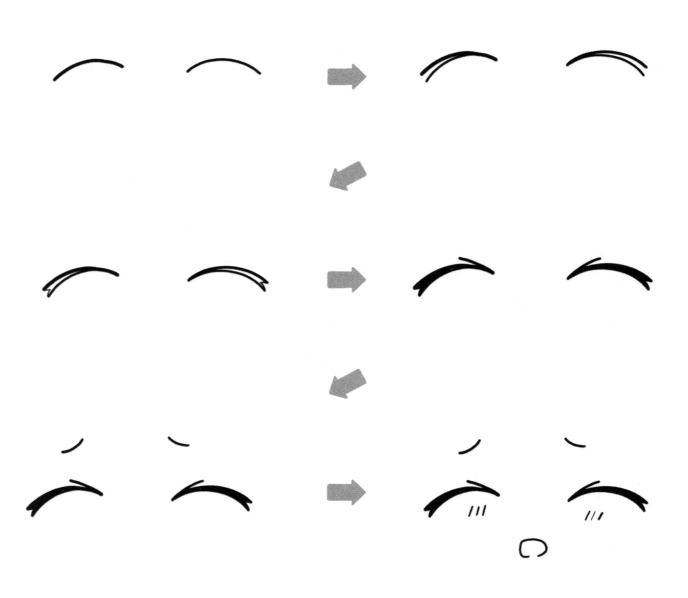

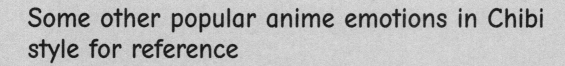

Some other popular anime emotions in Chibi style for reference

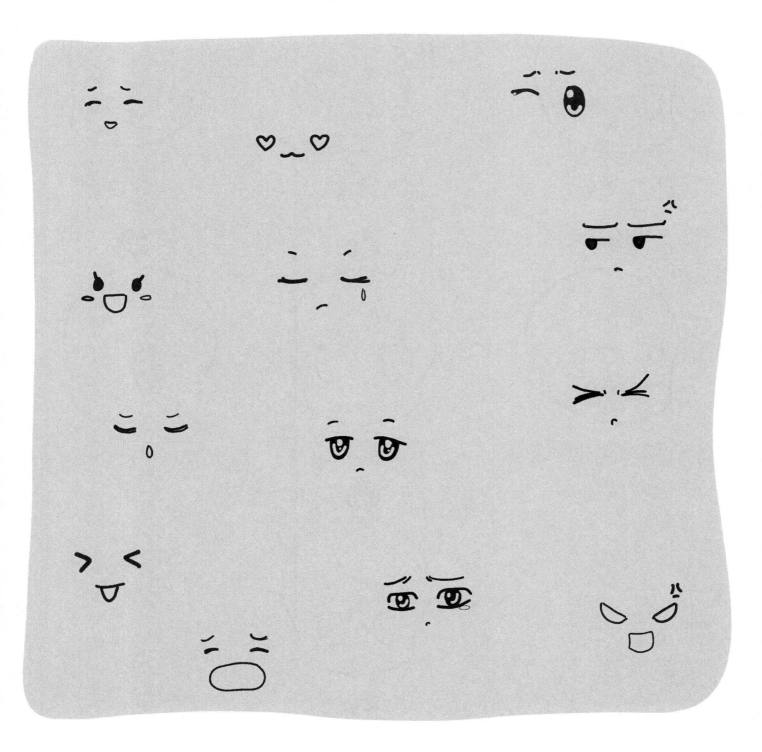

The Face's Angles

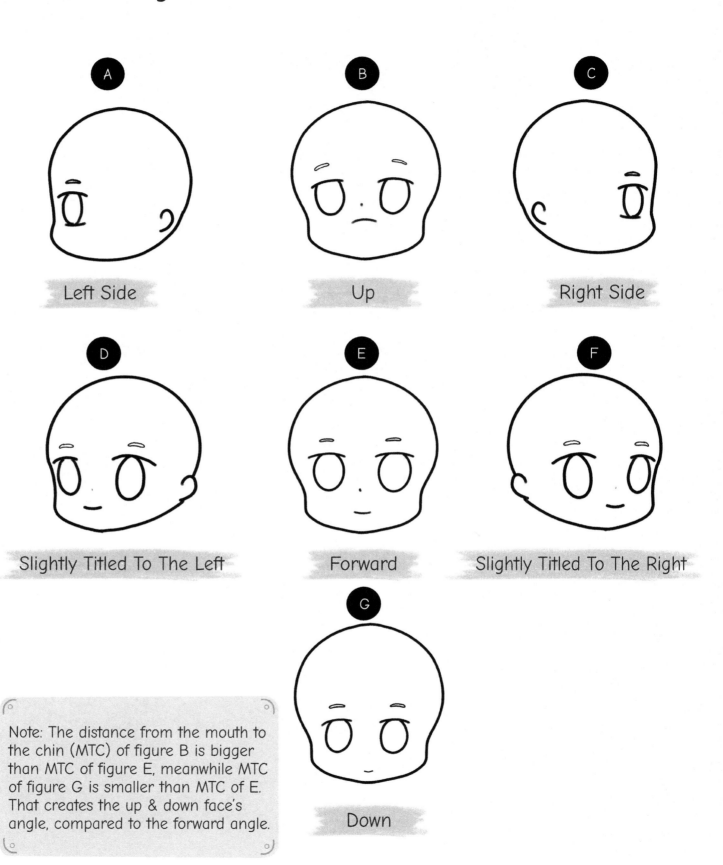

A — Left Side

B — Up

C — Right Side

D — Slightly Titled To The Left

E — Forward

F — Slightly Titled To The Right

G — Down

Note: The distance from the mouth to the chin (MTC) of figure B is bigger than MTC of figure E, meanwhile MTC of figure G is smaller than MTC of E. That creates the up & down face's angle, compared to the forward angle.

Up

Step 1:
Draw a circle.
Draw an arc line
that divide the
circle into 3:1 ratio
vertically

Step 2:
Draw the left
side cheek

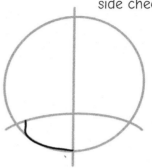

Step 3:
Draw the right side
cheek

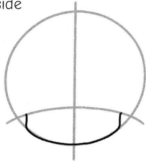

Step 4:
Draw the left
side temple and
forehead

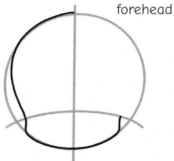

Step 5:
Draw the right side
temple and forehead

Step 6:
Add the eyes, nose
and mouth.

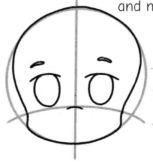

Notice: the distance from
mouth to chin is bigger
compared to the forward
face angle.

Step 1:
Draw a circle.
Draw an arc line
that divide the
circle into 3:1 ratio
vertically

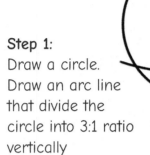

Step 2:
Draw the cheek

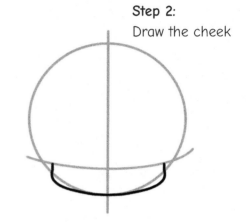

Step 3:
Draw the temples
and forehead

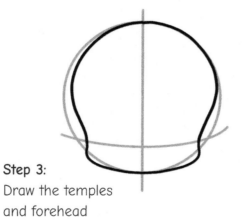

Step 4:
Add the eyes, nose
and mouth

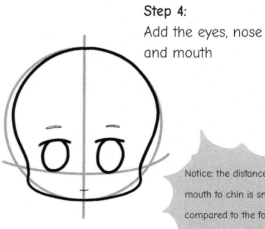

Notice: the distance from
mouth to chin is smaller
compared to the forward
face angle.

Left Side

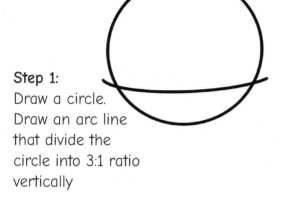

Step 1:
Draw a circle.
Draw an arc line
that divide the
circle into 3:1 ratio
vertically

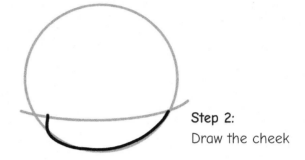

Step 2:
Draw the cheek

Step 3:
Draw the forehead

Step 4:
Draw the back
of the head

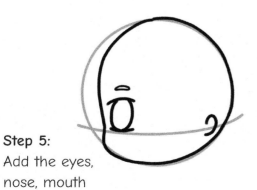

Step 5:
Add the eyes,
nose, mouth
and ears

Apply the same method
to draw the Right Side
face angle

27

Slightly Titled To The Left

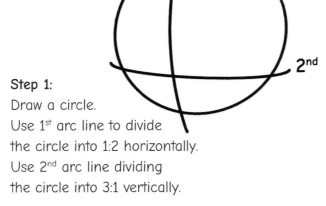

1st

2nd

Step 1:
Draw a circle.
Use 1st arc line to divide
the circle into 1:2 horizontally.
Use 2nd arc line dividing
the circle into 3:1 vertically.

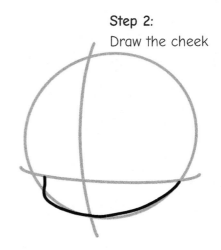

Step 2:
Draw the cheek

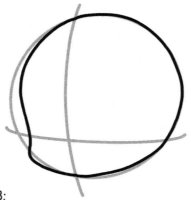

Step 3:
Draw the forehead

Step 4:
Add the eyes, nose
and mouth. .

Apply the same method
to draw the Slightly Titled
To The Right face angle

Notice to draw the
left eye smaller than
the right eye

The Hairstyles

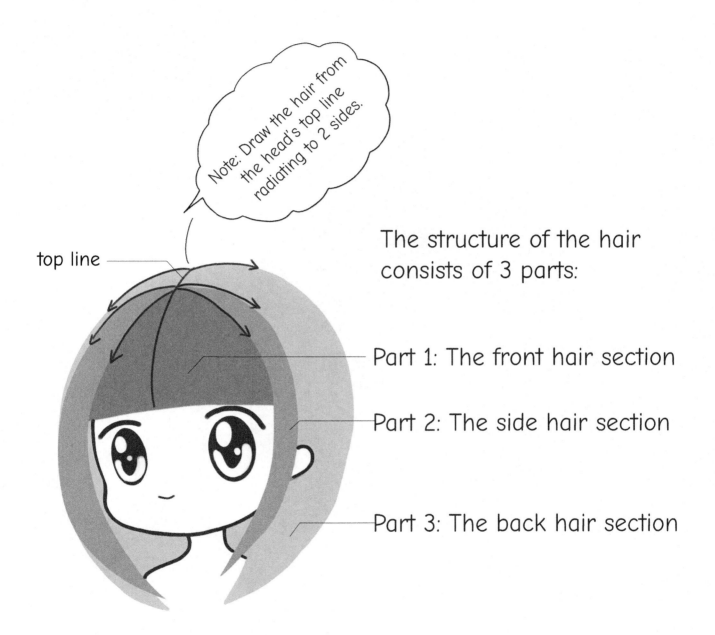

Note: Draw the hair from the head's top line radiating to 2 sides.

top line

The structure of the hair consists of 3 parts:

Part 1: The front hair section

Part 2: The side hair section

Part 3: The back hair section

The front hair section

The side hair section

The back hair section

Step By Step Drawing Tutorial: Basic Hairstyles

Cute Bob With Topknot

Step 1:
Draw the basic head
(see P. 28)

Step 2:
Draw the forehead hair

Step 3:
Continue to draw the forehead
hair using small arc lines

Step 4:
Draw the right side hair

Step 5:
Draw the left side hair

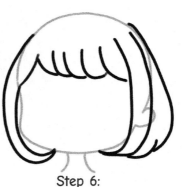

Step 6:
Draw the back hair

Step 7:
Draw the top hair that
covers the head's chop

Step 8:
Draw the hair behind
the nape

Step 9:
Draw the cute topknot
at the right side

Step 10:
Add the eyes,
eyebrows and mouth

Step 11:
Coloring

Step 1:
Draw the basic head
(see P. 28)

Step 2:
Draw the forehead hair

Step 3:
Continue to draw the forehead
hair using small arc lines

Step 4:
Draw the shape of
the side hair using S-line

Step 5:
Use the C-line to
finish drawing side hair

Step 6:
Draw the initial line
of the back hair

Step 7:
Use C-line to finish
drawing the back hair

Step 8:
Draw the top of the hair

Step 9:
Using small C-lines to
finish the whole hairstyle

Step 10:
Add the eyes,
eyebrows and mouth

Step 11:
Coloring

Shoulder Length Bob With Straight Bangs

Step 1:
Draw the basic head
(see P. 28)

Step 2:
Draw the initial L-shape
for the forehead hair

Step 3:
Finish drawing the forehead
hair using L-shape line

Step 4:
Draw the shape of
the side hair using S-line

Step 5:
Use the C-lines to finish
drawing the left side hair&
a part of the right frontal side hair

Step 6:
Draw the initial line of the
right back side hair

Step 7:
Use small C-lines to finish
drawing the back-right side hair

Step 8:
Draw the top of the hair

Step 9:
Using small C-lines to
finish the back hair section

Step 10:
Add the eyes,
eyebrows and mouth

Step 11:
Coloring

Step 1:
Draw the basic head
(see P. 28)

Step 2:
Draw the initial L-shape
for the forehead hair

Step 3:
Finish drawing the forehead
hair using L-shape line

Step 4:
Draw the shape of
the right front side hair

Step 5:
Draw the shape of
the left front side hair

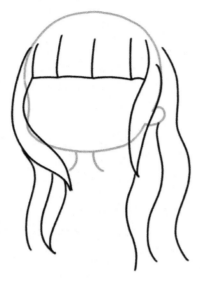

Step 6:
Using wavy lines to make
the look of both side hair

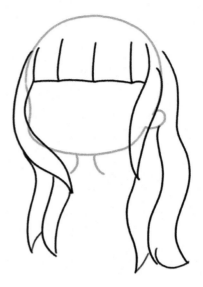

Step 7:
Complete the first part
of the long side hair

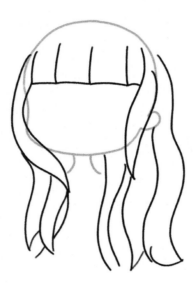

Step 8:
Add more wavy lines
to the long hair part

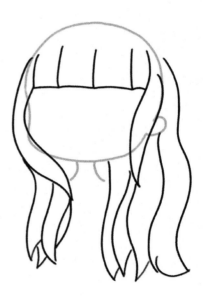

Step 9:
Finish the long hair part

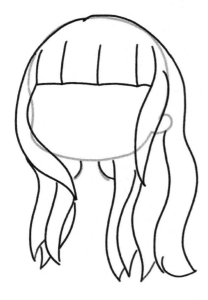

Step 10:

Draw the top of the hair

Step 11:

Add the eyes,
eyebrows and mouth

Step 12:

Coloring

Step 1:
Draw the basic head
(see P. 28)

Step 2:
Draw the initial curve lines
of the forehead hair section

Step 3:
Finish drawing the
choppy forehead

Step 4:
Draw the right side hair

Step 5:
Draw the left side hair

Step 6:
Draw the initial shape of the
right side tying twisted hair

Step 7:
Finish the first part of of the
right side tying twisted hair

Step 8:
Continue making the right side
tying twisted hair using a wavy line

Step 9:
Add another wavy line

Step 10:
Finish the right side
tying twisted hair

Step 11:
Draw the initial shape of the
left side tying twisted hair

Step 12:
Finish the first part of of the
left side tying twisted hair

Step 13:
Continue making the left side
tying twisted hair using a wavy line

Step 14:
Finish the left side
tying twisted hair

Step 15:
Draw the top of the hair

Step 16:
Add the eyes,
eyebrows and mouth

Step 17:
Coloring

Step 1:
Draw the basic head
(see P. 28)

Step 2:
Draw the initial L-shape
for the forehead hair

Step 3:
Finish drawing the
choppy forehead

Step 4:
Draw the right side hair

Step 5:
Draw the left side hair

Step 6:
Add the back hair
to the right side

Step 7:
Draw the top of the hair

Step 8:
Draw the shape of the bun

Step 9:
Add inner curve line to the bun

Step 10:
Using C-line to finish the look of the bun

Step 11:
Add the eyes,
eyebrows and mouth

Step 12:
Coloring

Double Bun

Step 1:
Draw the basic head
(see P. 28)

Step 2:
Draw the initial wavy lines
for the forehead hair

Step 3:
Adding straight lines
to the forehead hair

Step 4:
Complete the left part
of the forehead hair

Step 5:
Draw the initial line of the
right side forehead hair

Step 6:
Finish the whole
forehead hair

Step 7:
Draw the left side hair

Step 8:
Add the double bun
to the top of the hair

Step 9:
Finish the hairstyle

Step 10:
Add the eyes,
eyebrows and mouth

Step 11:
Coloring

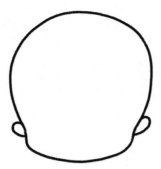

Step 1:
Draw the basic head
(see P. 25)

Step 2:
Draw the initial C-lines
for the forehead hair

Step 3:
Continue drawing the forehead
hair with the flipped C-lines

Step 4:
Draw the double side hair

Step 5:
Draw the top of the hair

Step 6:
Draw the initial straight line
of the left twisted braid

Step 7:
Complete the top part of
the left side twisted braid

Step 8:
Draw the initial lines of
the right side twisted braid

Step 9:
Complete the top part of
the right side twisted braid

Step 10:
Adding the tails

Step 11:
Add the eyes,
eyebrows and mouth

Step 12:
Coloring

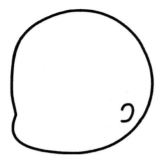

Step 1:
Draw the basic head
(see P. 27)

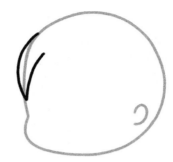

Step 2:
Draw the forehead hair

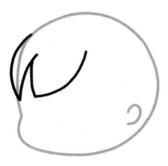

Step 3:
Draw the side hair

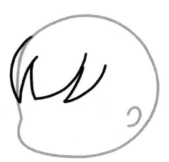

Step 4:
Adding another side hair part

Step 5:
Draw the initial shape
of the back hair

Step 6:
Complete the first part of the back hair

Step 7:

Draw the top of the hair

Step 8:

Draw the bow & initial
part of the ponytail

Step 9:

Use zic-zac line to continue
drawing the ponytail

Step 10:

Complete the ponytail

Step 11:

Add the eyes,
eyebrows and mouth

Step 12:

Coloring

Long Messy Fringe

Step 1:
Draw the basic head
(see P. 28)

Step 2:
Draw the initial lines
of the forehead hair

Step 3:
Continue drawing the forehead

Step 4:
Complete the forehead hair

Step 5:
Draw the right side hair

Step 6:
Draw the left side hair

Step 7:
Draw the top-right back hair

Step 8:
Draw the bottom-right back hair

Step 9:
Create the realistic look
on the top of the hair

Step 10:
Complete the top
part of the hair

Step 11:
Add the eyes,
eyebrows and mouth

Step 12:
Coloring

Long Side Part Fringe

Step 1:
Draw the basic head
(see P. 28)

Step 2:
Draw the forehead hair

Step 3:
Draw the right side hair

Step 4:
Draw the initial line
of the left side hair

Step 5:
Complete the left
side hair section

Step 6:
Using a C-line to fill the space
between left side hair and
forehead hair section

Step 7:
Complete the forehead
hair section

Step 8:
Draw the intial shape
of the right side hair

Step 9:
Complete drawing
the right side hair

Step 10:
Draw the top of the hair

Step 11:
Add the eyes,
eyebrows and mouth

Step 12:
Coloring

Step 1:
Draw the basic head
(see P. 28)

Step 2:
Draw the forehead hair

Step 3:
Draw the initial shape
of the top-right part of the hair

Step 4:
Continue drawing the
top-right part of the hair

Step 5:
Draw the bottom-right
part of the hair

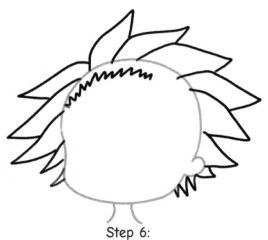

Step 6:
Draw the left side hair

Step 7:
Use a C-line to connect the
left side and the right side hair

Step 8:
Draw the initial shape of
the middle-right side hair

Step 9:
Complete the middle
-right side hair

Step 10:
Add the eyes,
eyebrows and mouth

Step 11:
Coloring

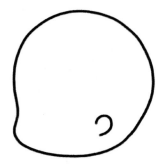

Step 1:
Draw the basic head
(see P. 27)

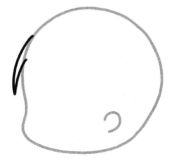

Step 2:
Draw the initial part
of the forehead hair

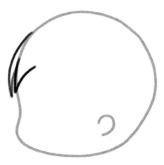

Step 3:
Continue drawing the
forehead hair

Step 4:
Drawing the intial
shape of the side hair

Step 5:
Continue drawing the side hair

Step 6:
Complete the side hair
part that covers the ears

Step 7:
Draw the back of the hair

Step 8:
Draw the top of the hair

Step 9:
Complete the hairstyle

Step 10:
Add the eyes,
eyebrows and mouth

Step 11:
Coloring

Arms

Introduction

The arms' structure consists of 3 parts: biceps, forearm, and hands.

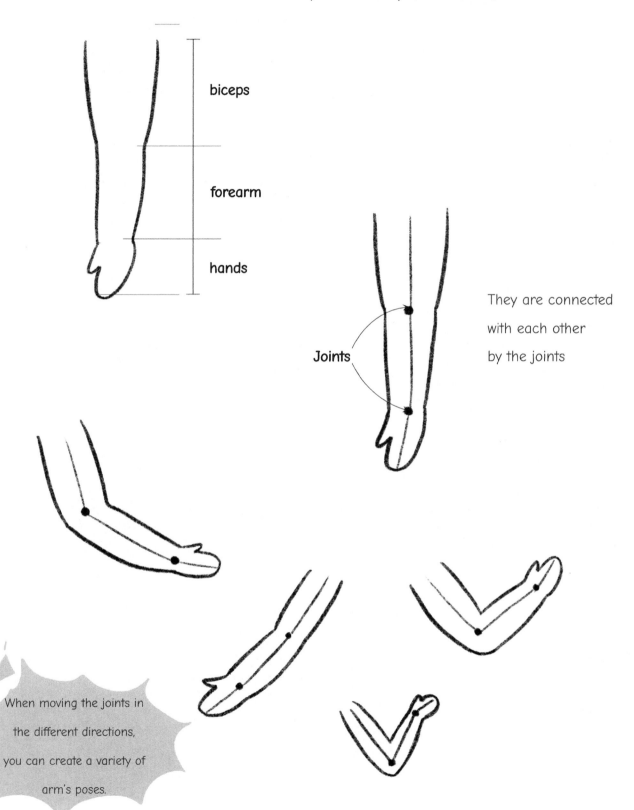

biceps

forearm

hands

Joints

They are connected
with each other
by the joints

When moving the joints in
the different directions,
you can create a variety of
arm's poses.

The arm: Step by step drawing tutorial

Step 1:
Draw a long
oval for the bicep

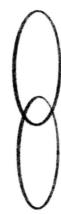

Step 2:
Draw a longer
oval for the forearm

Step 3:
Draw a circle
for the hand

Step 4:
Draw clearly the arc
lines to finish the shape
of bicep and forearm.

Notice: Those lines
should be able to create
a chubby, cute shape.

Step 5:
Draw the hand,
just simple like this

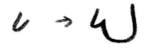

Legs

☞ Introduction

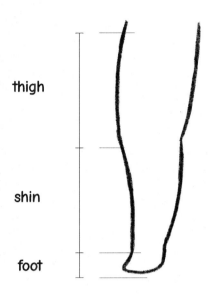

thigh

shin

foot

The legs' structure consists of the thigh, shin and foot

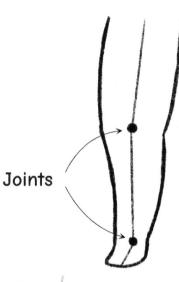

Joints

They are connected with each other by the joints

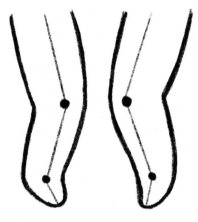

When moving the joints in the different directions, you can create a variety of leg's poses.

The leg: Step by step drawing tutorial

Step 1:
Draw a fat long
oval for the thigh

Step 2:
Draw a thin long
oval for the shin

Step 3:
Draw a circle
for the foot

Step 4:
Using clear arc lines
to finish the shape of
thigh and shin.

Notice to make them look
chubby and cute.

Step 5:
Finish the foot

The Torso Shapes

Introduction

There are two types of torso shapes: avocado and bean.

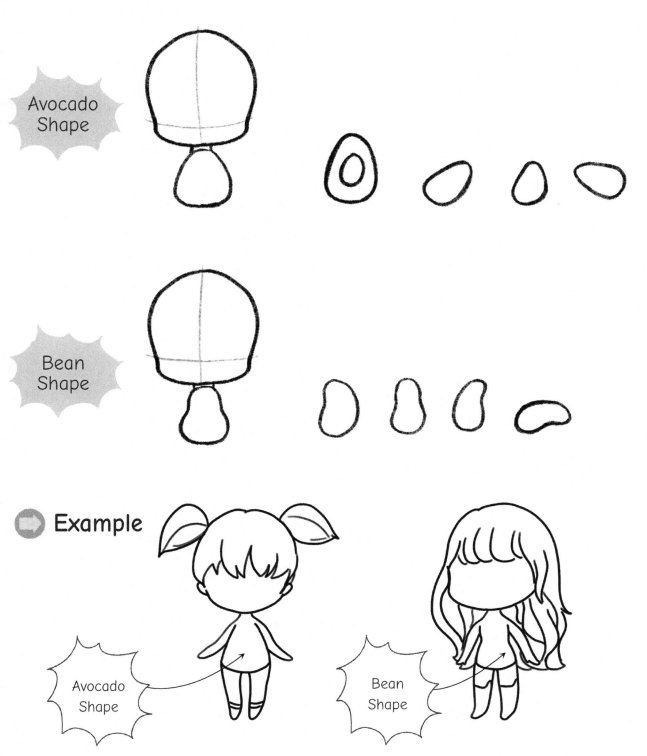

Avocado
Shape

Bean
Shape

Example

Avocado
Shape

Bean
Shape

POSES

How to draw a pose

Notice that there are moving joints on a body.

When moving the joints, you are able to create a variety of different poses.

The basic pose

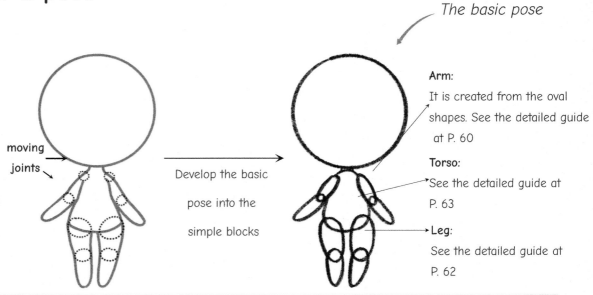

moving joints

Develop the basic pose into the simple blocks

Arm:
It is created from the oval shapes. See the detailed guide at P. 60

Torso:
See the detailed guide at P. 63

Leg:
See the detailed guide at P. 62

From the basic pose, we can create different poses by moving the joints like this

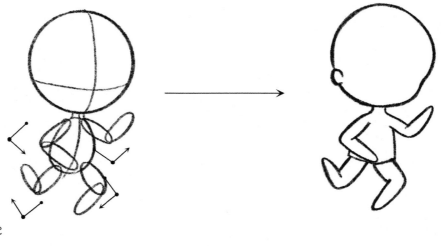

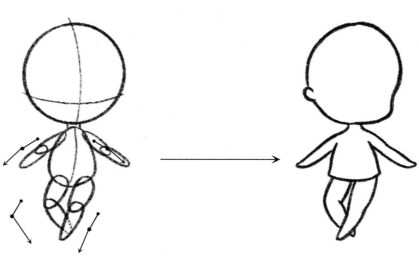

14 Popular Poses

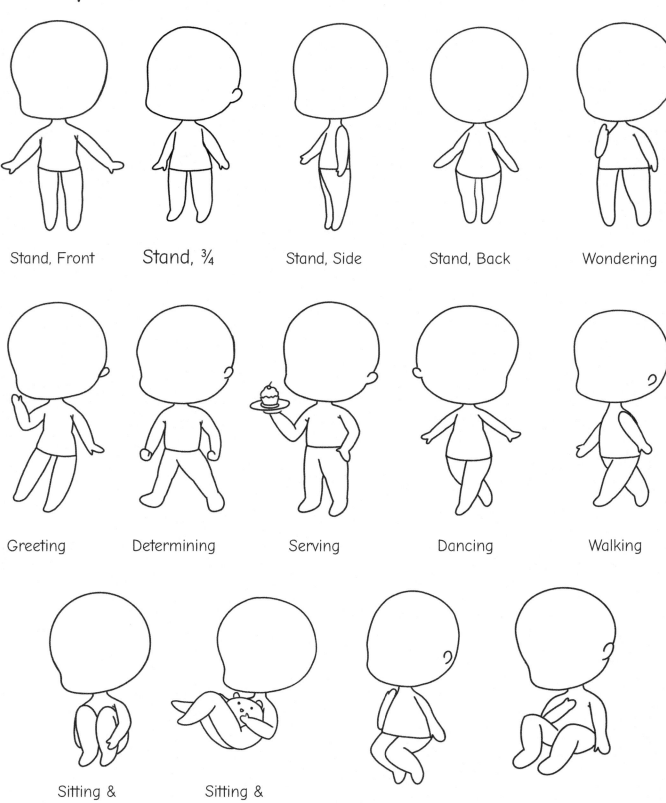

Stand, Front   Stand, ¾   Stand, Side   Stand, Back   Wondering

Greeting   Determining   Serving   Dancing   Walking

Sitting &
Hugging Knees

Sitting &
Leaning Back

Sitting, Side   Sitting, Holding Chest

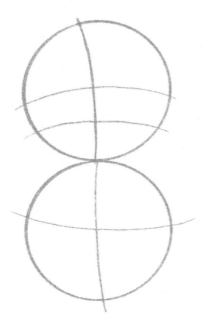

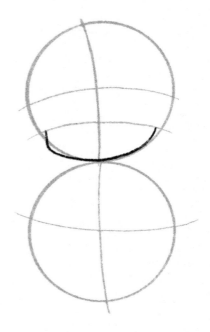

Step 1:

Draw 2 similar size circles.
Divide them into basic
proportion (see P. 9)

Step 2:

Draw the cheek

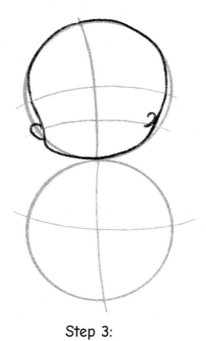

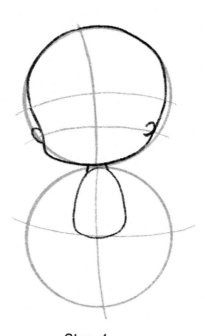

Step 3:

Draw the forehead and ears

Step 4:

Draw the torso's
container

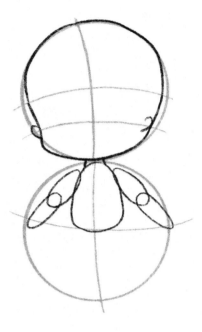

Step 5:

Draw the arms' containers

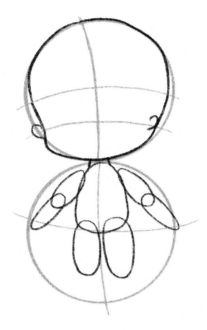

Step 6:

Draw the thighs' containers

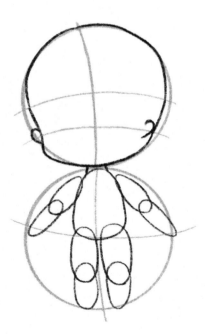

Step 7:

Finish the containers

of the legs

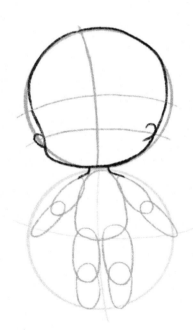

Step 8:

Draw the neck & shoulders

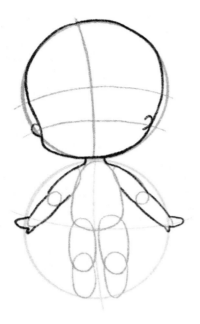

Step 9:

Finish the whole

arms & hands

Step 10:

Finish the torso part.

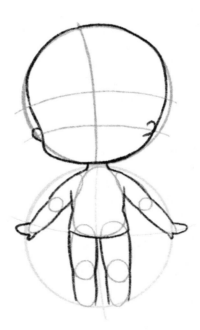

Step 11:

Finish the legs

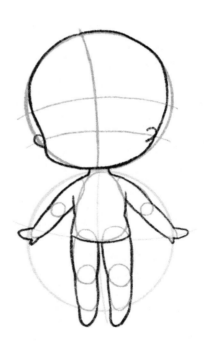

Step 12:

Finish the feet.

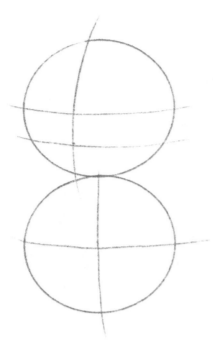

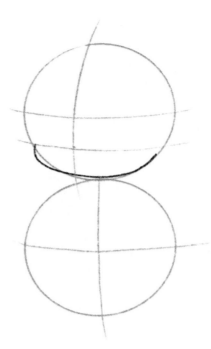

Step 1:

Draw 2 similar size circles.
Divide them into basic
proportion (see P. 9)

Step 2:

Draw the cheek

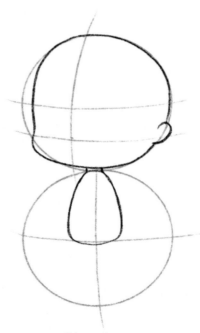

Step 3:

Draw the forehead and ears

Step 4:

Draw the torso's
container

Step 5:

Draw the arms' containers

Step 6:

Draw the legs' containers

Step 7:

Draw the neck

Step 8:

Finish drawing the

arm and the hand

Step 9:

Finish the torso part

Step 10:

Draw the legs

Step 11:

Draw the feet

☙ Stand, Side.

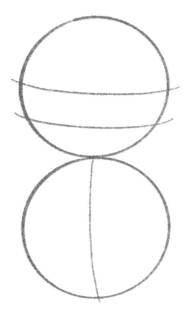

Step 1:

Draw 2 similar size circles.
Divide them into basic
proportion (see P. 9)

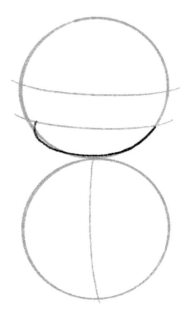

Step 2:

Draw the cheek

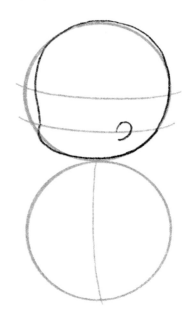

Step 3:

Draw the forehead and ears

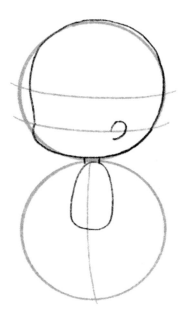

Step 4:

Draw the torso's
container

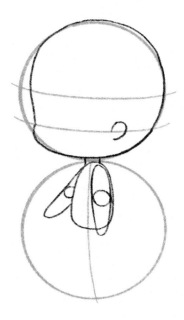

Step 5:

Draw the arms'
containers

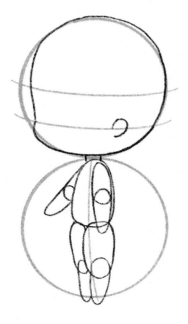

Step 6:

Draw the legs'
containers

Step 7:

Draw the neck

Step 8:

Draw the arms
and the hands

Step 9:

Finish the torso part

Step 10:

Draw the legs

Step 11:

Draw the feet

Stand, Back.

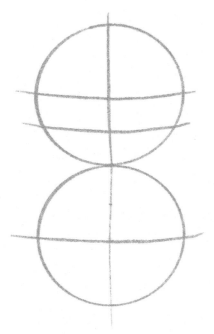

Step 1:

Draw 2 similar size circles.

Divide them into basic

proportion (see P. 9)

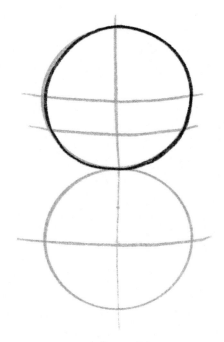

Step 2:

Draw the back of the

head using round shape

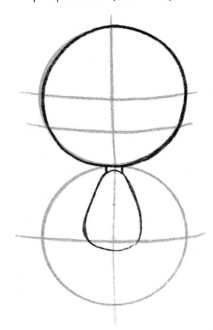

Step 3:

Draw the torso's

container

Step 4:

Draw the arms' container

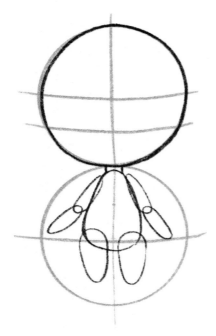

Step 5:

Draw the thighs'

containers

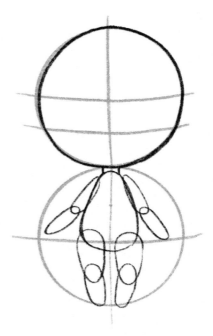

Step 6:

Finish drawing the

legs' containers

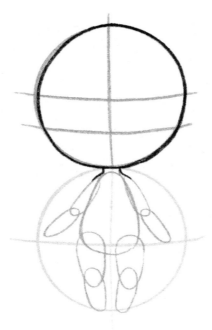

Step 7:

Draw the neck

and the shoulder

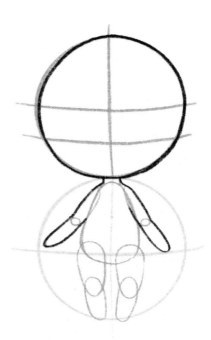

Step 8:

Draw the arms

and the hands

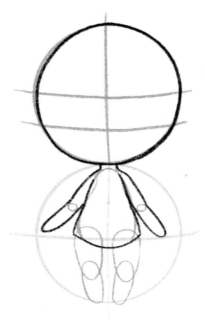

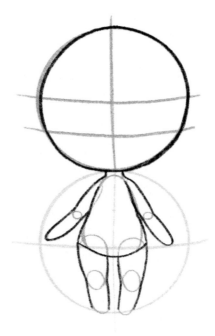

Step 9:

Finish drawing the torso

Step 10:

Draw the legs

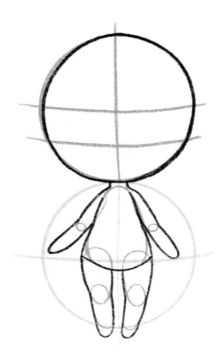

Step 11:

Draw the feet

77

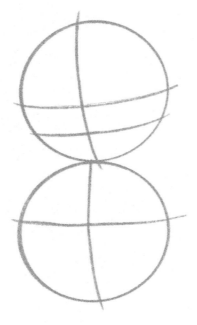

Step 1:

Draw 2 similar size circles.

Divide them into basic

proportion (see P. 9)

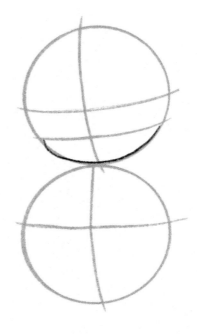

Step 2:

Draw the cheek

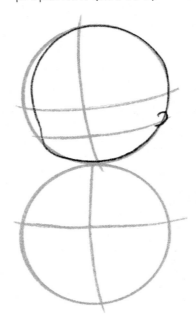

Step 3:

Draw the forehead and ears

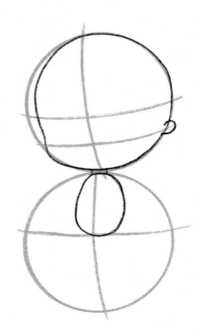

Step 4:

Draw the torso's container

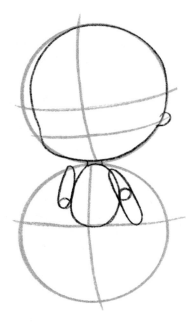

Step 5:

Draw the arms'

containers

Step 6:

Draw the legs'

containers

Step 7:

Draw the neck & shoulders

Step 8:

Draw the arms

and the hands

Step 9:

Finish drawing the torso

Step 10:

Draw the legs

Step 11:

Draw the feet

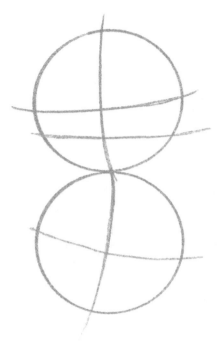

Step 1:

Draw 2 similar size circles.
Divide them into basic
proportion (see P. 9)

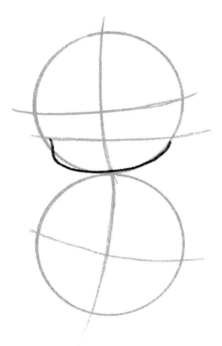

Step 2:

Draw the cheek

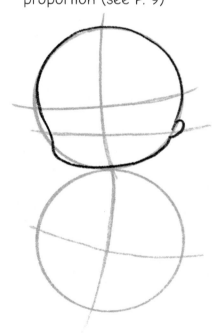

Step 3:

Draw the forehead and ears

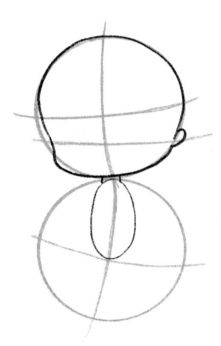

Step 4:

Draw the torso's
container

81

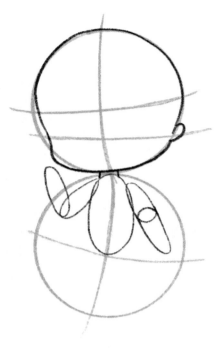

Step 5:

Draw the arms'

containers

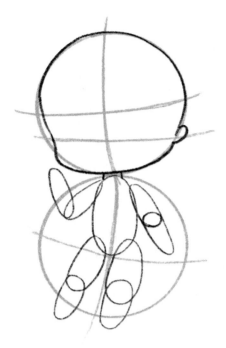

Step 6:

Draw the legs'

containers

Step 7:

Draw the neck &

shoulders

Step 8:

Draw the arms

and the hands

Step 9:

Finish drawing the torso

Step 10:

Draw the legs

Step 11:

Draw the feet

Determined

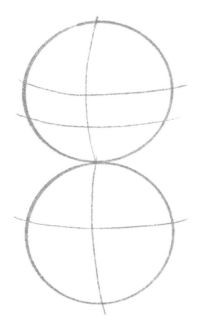

Step 1:

Draw 2 similar size circles.
Divide them into basic
proportion (see P. 9)

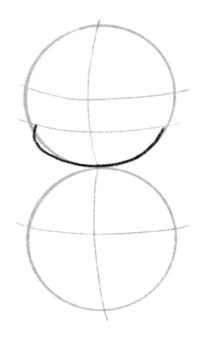

Step 2:

Draw the cheek

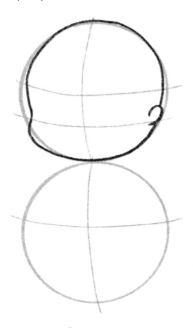

Step 3:

Draw the forehead
and ears

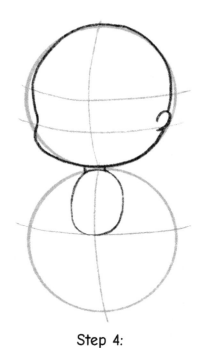

Step 4:

Draw the torso's
container

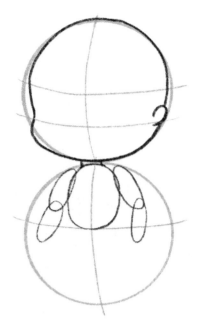

Step 5:

Draw the arms' containers

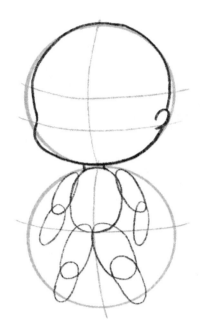

Step 6:

Draw the legs' containers

Step 7:

Draw the neck

and the shoulders

Step 8:

Draw the arms

Step 9:

Draw the fists

Step 10:

Finish drawing

the torso

Step 11:

Finish drawing the legs

Step 12:

Finish drawing the feet.

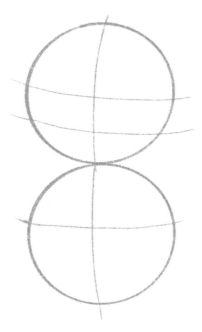

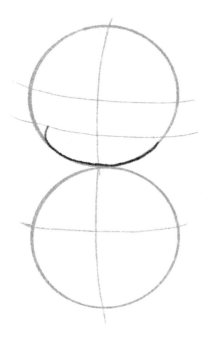

Step 1:

Draw 2 similar size circles.
Divide them into basic
proportion (see P. 9)

Step 2:

Draw the cheek

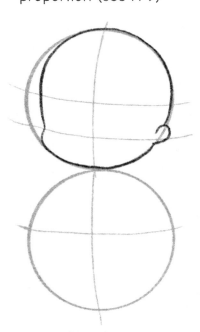

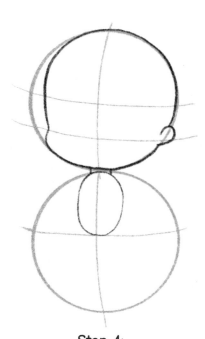

Step 3:

Draw the forehead
and ears

Step 4:

Draw the torso's
container

Step 5:

Draw the arms' containers

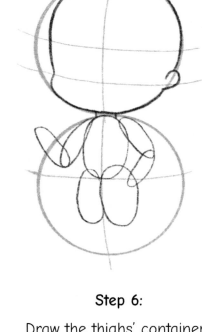

Step 6:

Draw the thighs' containers

Step 7:

Draw the containers

of the legs

Step 8:

Draw the neck,

shoulders, and the arms

Step 9:

Draw the hands - one is serving

a cake, other is holding the hip

Step 10:

Finish the torso.

Step 11:

Draw the legs

Step 12:

Draw the feet.

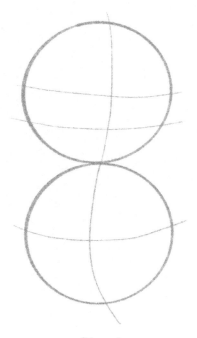

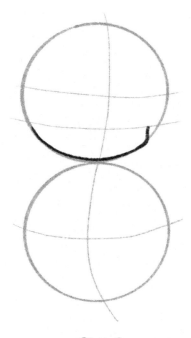

Step 1:

Draw 2 similar size circles.
Divide them into basic
proportion (see P. 9)

Step 2:

Draw the cheek

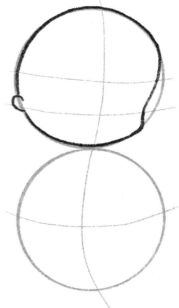

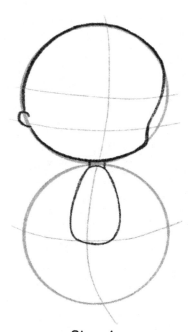

Step 3:

Draw the forehead and ears

Step 4:

Draw the torso's
container

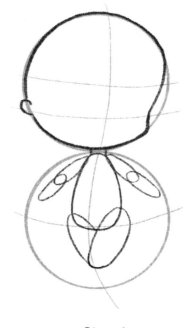

Step 5:

Draw the arms' containers

Step 6:

Draw the thighs' containers

Step 7:

Finish drawing the

containers of the legs

Step 8:

Draw the neck

and the shoulders.

Step 9:

Draw the arms

and the hands

Step 10:

Finish drawing

the torso

Step 11:

Draw the legs

Step 12:

Draw the feet.

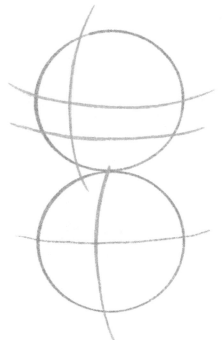

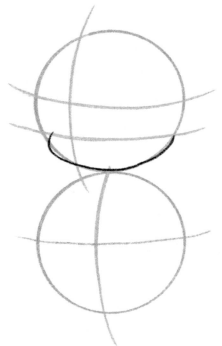

Step 1:

Draw 2 similar size circles.
Divide them into basic
proportion (see P. 9)

Step 2:

Draw the cheek

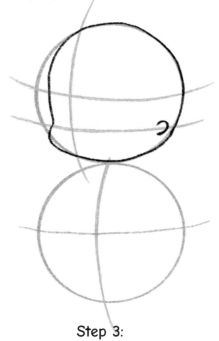

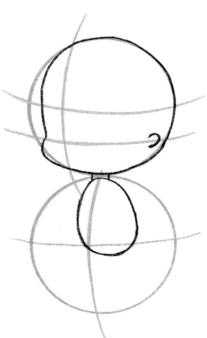

Step 3:

Draw the forehead and ears

Step 4:

Draw the torso's
container

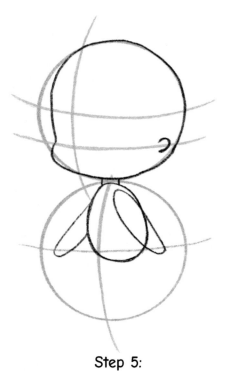

Step 5:

Draw the arms' containers

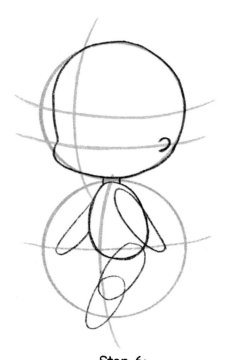

Step 6:

Draw the left

leg's container

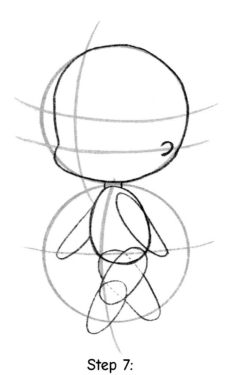

Step 7:

Draw the right leg's container

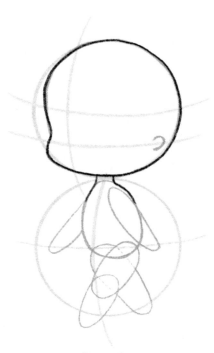

Step 8:

Draw the neck

& the shoulders

Step 9:

Draw the whole

arms & hands

Step 10:

Draw the torso

Step 11:

Draw the left leg & foot

Step 12:

Draw the right leg & foot

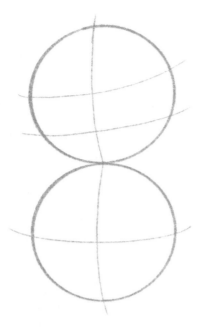

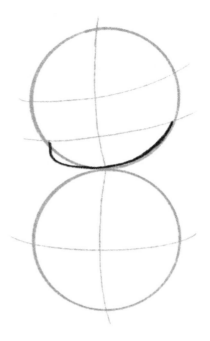

Step 1:

Draw 2 similar size circles.
Divide them into basic
proportion (see P. 9)

Step 2:

Draw the cheek

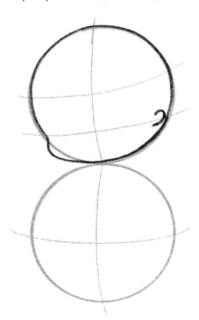

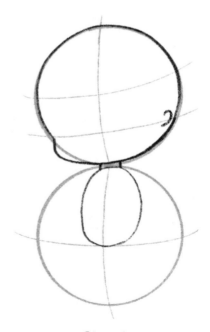

Step 3:

Draw the forehead
and ears

Step 4:

Draw the torso's
container

Step 5:

Draw the legs' containers

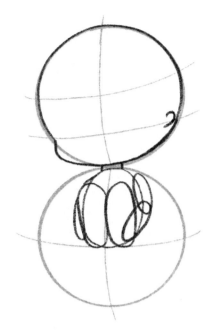

Step 6:

Draw the arms' containers

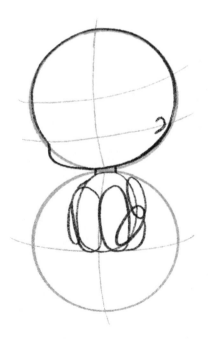

Step 7:

Draw the butt's container

Step 8:

Draw the neck
& shoulders

Step 9:

Draw the whole

arms & hands

Step 10:

Draw the legs.

Step 11:

Draw the feet

Step 12:

Draw the butt

Sitting, Leaning Back

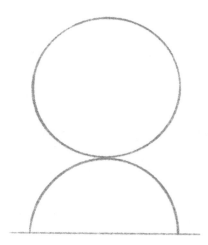

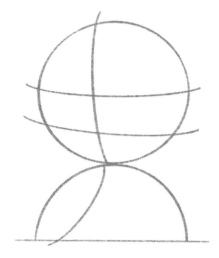

Step 1:

Draw 2 similar size circles.
Divide the bottom circle into two
equal parts using horizontal line,
then erase the bottom part

Step 2:

Divide the containers
using basic proportion
(see P. 9)

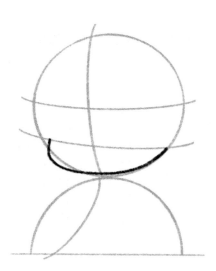

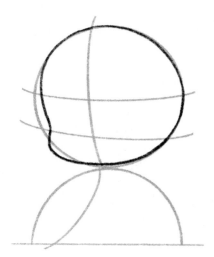

Step 3:

Draw the cheek

Step 4:

Draw the forehead

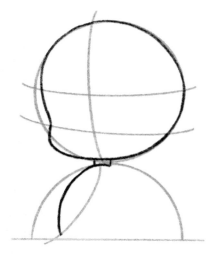

Step 5:

Draw the neck container
& the initial line of
torso container

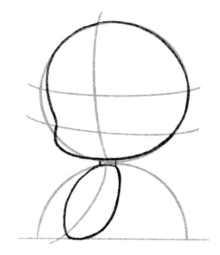

Step 6:

Finish drawing the
torso's container

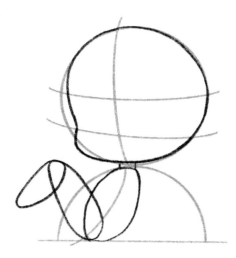

Step 7:

Draw the container
of the left leg

Step 8:

Add the container
of the right leg

Step 9:

Draw the arm's container

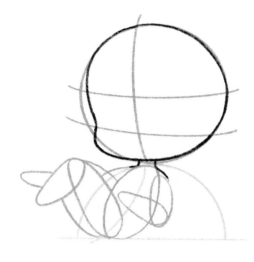

Step 10:

Draw the neck & the shoulders

Step 11:

Draw the stuffed

bear

Step 12:

Draw the arms

Step 13:

Draw the hands

Step 14:

Draw the left

leg & foot.

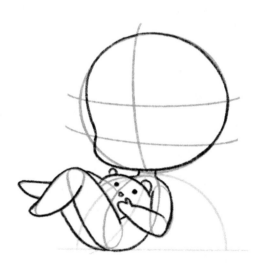

Step 15:

Draw the right

leg & foot

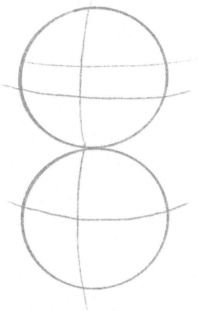

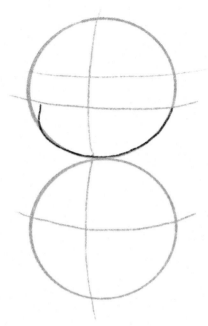

Step 1:

Draw 2 similar size circles.

Divide them into basic

proportion (see P. 9)

Step 2:

Draw the cheek

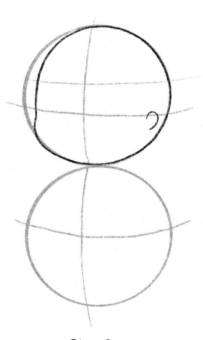

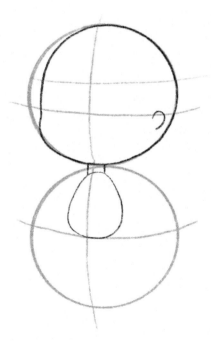

Step 3:

Draw the forehead

and ears

Step 4:

Draw the torso's

container

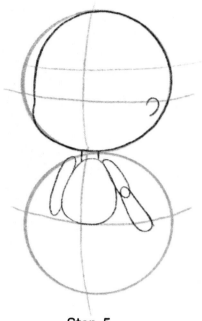

Step 5:

Draw the arms'
containers

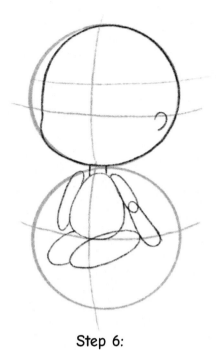

Step 6:

Draw the thighs'
containers

Step 7:

Finish drawing the
containers of the
legs

Step 8:

Draw the neck
& the shoulders

Step 9:

Draw the whole

arms & hands

Step 10:

Draw the torso

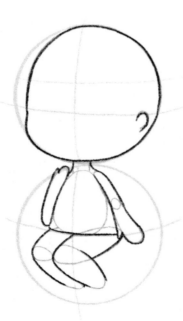

Step 11:

Draw the legs

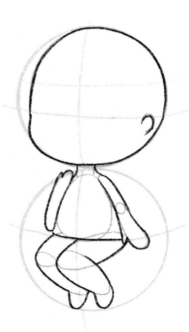

Step 12:

Draw the feet.

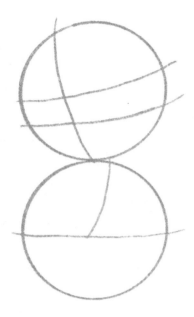

Step 1:

Draw 2 similar size circles.

Divide them into basic

proportion (see P. 9)

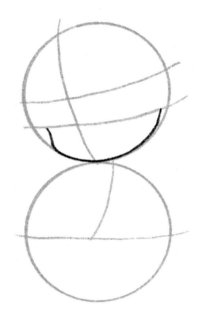

Step 2:

Draw the cheek

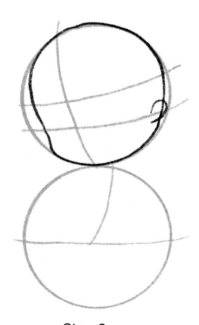

Step 3:

Draw the forehead

and ears

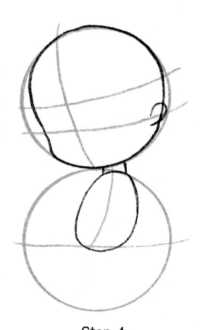

Step 4:

Draw the torso's

container

Step 5:

Draw the thighs'

containers

Step 6:

Draw the legs'

containers

Step 7:

Draw the containers

of the arms

Step 8:

Draw the neck

& shoulders

Step 9:

Draw the whole

arms & hands

Step 10:

Draw the torso & legs.

Step 11:

Draw the feet

CLOTHING

Clothing in Chibi plays an important role in creating the traits of character. Mastering the ability to draw the popular anime clothing in Chibi style will allow you to give your character a more realistic & soulful look.

Girl's Uniform

Step 1:
Draw the collar

Step 2:
Draw the tie bow

Step 3:
Draw the lace
above the collar

Step 4:
Draw the body
of the uniform

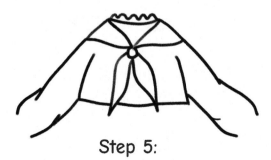

Step 5:
Draw the sleeves

Step 6:

Draw the cuffs

Step 7:

Draw the lapel

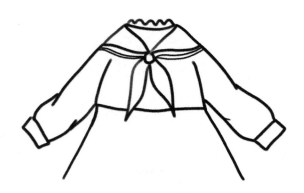

Step 8:

Draw the skirt's sides

Step 9:

Draw the skirt's wave

Step 10:

Draw straight lines from the
top of the waves to the belt line

Wool Dress

Step 1:
Draw the collar

Step 2:
Draw the dress's body

Step 3:
Draw the dress's
sleeves

Step 4:
Draw the cuffs

Step 5:
Add the strings & the
wool balls. You're done!

Winter Dress & Scarf

Step 1:
Draw the top
of the scarf

Step 2:
Add the extra
lines as above

Step 3:
Finish the shape of
the scarf's top

Step 4:
Draw the tail of the scarf

Step 5:
Finish the scarf by adding
arc lines as above

Step 6:
Draw the body
of the winter dress

Step 7:

Add the sleeves

Step 8:

Draw the cuffs

Step 9:

Finish the winter dress
by adding decorated details

Short Sleeve Shirt & Shorts

Step 1:
Draw the collar

Step 2:
Draw the shirt's body

Step 3:
Draw the short
sleeves

Step 4:
Draw the placket

Step 5:
Add buttons onto the placket

Step 6:

Add decoration details
to the placket

Step 7:

Draw the sides and middle
lines of the shorts

Step 8:

Draw the leg opening

Step 9:

Add an arc line on the top
of the leg opening part

Cardigan, Turtleneck & A Line Skirt

Step 1:
Draw the collar
of the turtleneck

Step 2:
Draw the cardigan's
side seam

Step 3:
Add the sleeves
to the cardigan

Step 4:
Draw the lapel

Step 5:
Draw the front bottom
part of the cardigan

Step 6:
Draw the bottom
line of the turtleneck

Step 7:
Draw the side of
the A line skirt

Step 8:
Draw the bottom of
the A line skirt

Step 9:
Add details to make
the skirt more realistic

Pajama

Step 1:
Draw the top of
the collar

Step 2:
Finish the collar

Step 3:
Draw the side seam
& the bottom line
of the shirt part

Step 4:
Add the short sleeves

Step 5:
Draw the side lines
of the pants

Step 6:
Draw the inner lines
of the pants

Step 7:
Draw the leg
opening

Step 8:
Add details to finish
the pajama

Turtleneck, Strap Skirt & Legging

Step 1:
Draw the collar

Step 2:
Add the sleeves

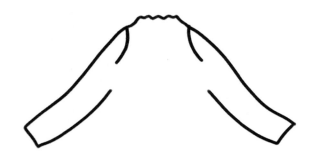

Step 3:
Draw the top two lines
of the strap skirt

Step 4:
Draw the shape of
the strap skirt

Step 5:
Finish the strap skirt

Step 6:

Draw the legging's side

Step 7:

Draw the legging's inner

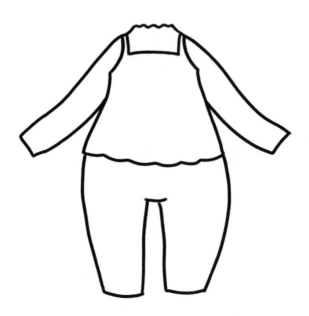

Step 8:

Draw the leg opening

Puff Sleeve Dress

Step 1:

Draw the collar

Step 2:

Draw the 2-wire

part of the dress

Step 3:

Draw a wave shape

under the wires

Step 4:

Add another wave

shape as above

Step 5:

Complete the first

part of the 2-wire skirt

Step 6:

Use straight line to

connect the top points

of the wave shape as above

Step 7:

Draw a bigger wave shape

Step 8:

Use straight line to connect

the top points of the

wave shape as above

Step 9:

Draw a big wave shape

Step 10:

Draw the straight

lines as above

Step 11:

From the top points of

the wave, draw the line

heading to the belt part

Step 12:

Draw the shape of the sleeves

Step 13:

Draw the cuff

Step 14:

Add the bows on the

sleeves to finish drawing the dress

Princess Dress

Step 1:
Draw the initial
shape of the collar

Step 2:
Finish drawing the collar

Step 3:
Draw the cape
on the shoulders

Step 4:
Draw the placket
and buttons

Step 5:
Draw the belt line

Step 6:
Draw the initial shape of
the skirt part of the dress

Step 7:

Add a wavy
line as above

Step 8:

Draw straight lines from
the top of the wave heading
to the belt line

Step 9:

Draw a wave shape
under the skirt part

Step 10:

Use small straight lines
to finish drawing the skirt
part of the dress

Step 11:

Draw the initial shape
of the sleeves

Step 12:

Draw the cuffs

Step 13:

Add details to the belt
part to make it
look more realistic

Step 14:

Add the decorated bows
to the princess dress

Short Sleeve T-Shirt

Step 1:
Draw the collar

Step 2:
Draw the initial shape
of the t-shirt's body

Step 3:
Add a straight line
to finish drawing the
t-shirt's body

Step 4:
Draw the short sleeves

Step 5:
Add details to make it
look more realistic

Trousers

Step 1:
Draw the trousers belt

Step 2:
Draw the initial shape
of the left trousers leg

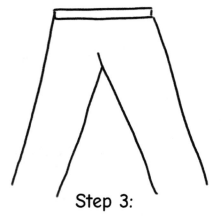

Step 3:
Draw the right
trousers leg

Step 4:
Draw the leg
opening

Step 5:
Add details to make
it look more realistic

Waistcoat & Shirt

Step 1:
Draw the bow tie

Step 2:
Draw the initial
shape of the waistcoat

Step 3:
Finish drawing
the waistcoat

Step 4:
Draw the lapel

Step 5:

Draw the tie

Step 6:

Add the button

Step 7:

Add the sleeves

Step 8:

Draw the cuff.
Finish drawing the set
of waistcoat & shirt

Boy's Uniform

Step 1:

Draw the bow tie

Step 2:

Draw the initial shape
of the uniform's body

Step 3:

Draw the sleeves

Step 4:

Draw the cuffs

Step 5:

Draw the lapel
of the sweater

Step 6:

Draw the tie

Step 7:

Add details to make the
set look more realistic

Hoodie

Step 1:
Draw the initial
shape of the collar

Step 2:
Draw the shoulders
part of the hoodie

Step 3:
Finish the hoodie's
collar

Step 4:
Draw the hoodie strips

Step 5:
Draw the initial part
of the hoodie's body

Step 6:
Draw the sleeves

Step 7:
Draw the cuffs

Step 8:
Add details to make the
hoodie look more realistic

HIGHLIGHTS & SHADOWS

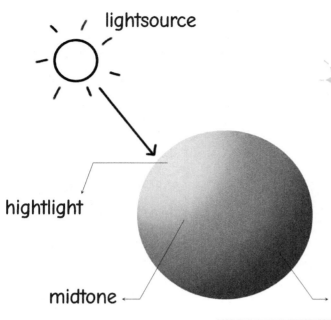

lightsource

hightlight

midtone

shadow

Highlight & shadow makes characters look more realistic.

Tips: Using 3 levels of color, from darkest to brightest to make shadows and highlights for the characters.

- The brightest one: highlight
- The average one: midtone
- The darkest one: shadow

At the ball above, highlight is the part that is the nearest to the lightsource, next to that is the midtones - neutral color part, and finally the shadow part.

Midtones
First we pick the main colors that we use for the characters. Those colors are midtones.

Add Shadow
Pick the darker and deeper color of midtones to use into the out of light area for creating the shadows.

Add Highlight
Pick the brightest color of midtones to use into the areas closest to the light source for creating the highlights

PRACTICES

Introduction: The Popular Characters

MIKASA

- Age: 8.
- Hobbies: Dancing and Singing.
- Characteristics: Extrovert, Energetic, Friendly.

NEZUKO

- Age: 10
- Hobbies: Playing Piano
- Characteristics: Caring, Sensitive & Kind.

SHINOBU

- Age: 9
- Hobbies: Cosplaying
- Characteristics: Mysterious, Charming, Inventive, Versatile.

SHANNON

- Age: 11
- Hobbies: Writing Poem
- Characteristics: Creative, Passionate & Altruistic.

KANAO

- Age: 13
- Hobbies: Traveling
- Characteristics: Dedicated, Honest & Loyal

JUNJOU

- Age: 12
- Hobbies: Reading Manga
- Characteristics: Observant, Practical & Aesthetic

SAIKI

- Age: 7
- Hobbies: Cooking & Baking
- Characteristics: Curious, Enthusiastic & Friendly

ALICE

- Age: 11
- Hobbies: Shopping
- Characteristics: Tolerant, Reliable & Charismatic

BOKU

- Age: 13
- Hobbies: Playing Volleyball
- Characteristics: Rational, Independent & Informed

JUDY

- Age: 14
- Hobbies: Jogging
- Characteristics: Determined, Objective

& imaginative

DANNY

- Age: 11.
- Hobbies: Rapping
- Characteristics: Quick Thinkers, Know

-ledgeable & Original

JACKSON

- Age: 13
- Hobbies: Making cakes
- Characteristics: Calm, Responsible & Dutiful

HUNTER

- Age: 10.
- Hobbies: Boxing
- Characteristics: Energetic, Powerful & Practical

YAIBA

- Age: 14
- Hobbies: Drawing
- Characteristics: Thoughtful, Generous & Creative

Step By Step Tutorial: The Popular Characters

MIKASA

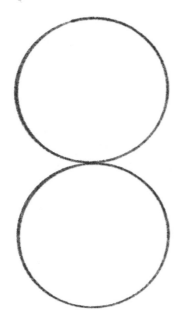

Draw 02 similar size circle

Divide the circles as the proportion described at P. 90

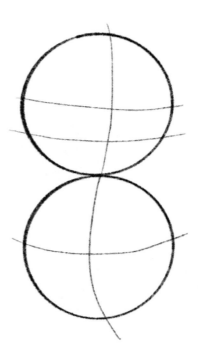

Finish the dance pose (see P. 90 - P. 92)

Add the Double Bun
hairstyle
(see P. 45 - P. 46)

Draw the Puff Sleeves
Dress (see P. 122 - P.123)

Add the eyes, eyebrows,
and mouth

Use brushed pen to finalize
the drawing and
erase the containers

Colorize the character

Use highlights & shadows
(see P. 135)

NEZUKO

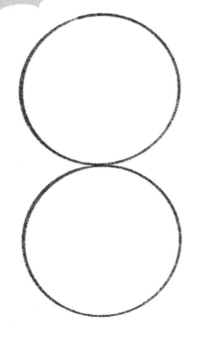

Draw 02 similar size circle

Divide the circles as the proportion described at P. 66

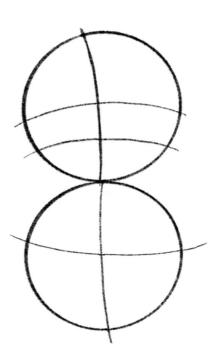

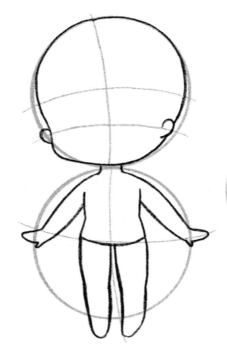

Draw the Stand, Front pose (see P. 66 - P. 68)

Draw the Thick Bangs With Double Rope Twisted Braid hairstyle (see P. 47 - P. 48)

Draw the Princess Dress (see P. 124 - P. 126)

Add the eyes, eyebrows, and mouth

Use brushed pen to finalize
the drawing and
erase the containers

Colorize the character

Use highlights & shadows
(see P. 135)

SHINOBU

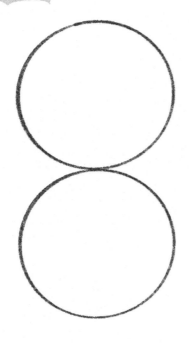

Draw 02 similar size circle

Divide the circles as the proportion described at P. 75

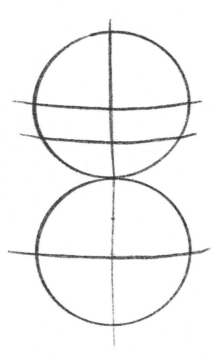

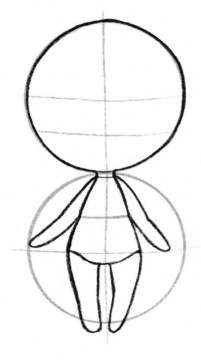

Draw the Stand, Back pose (see P. 75 - P. 77)

Draw the Cute Bob Hairstyle, Back View & sketch the Basic Dress

Use brushed pen to finish the draw and erase the containers

Add the shadows & highlight (see P. 135)

SHANNON

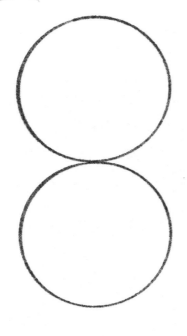

Draw 02 similar size circle

Divide the circles as the proportion described at P. 103

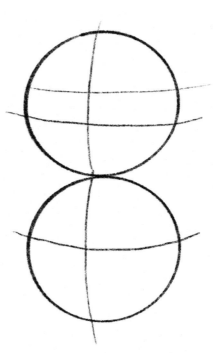

Draw the Sitting, Side pose (see P. 103 - P. 105)

Draw the Long Wavy Hair
With Straight Bangs
(see P. 37 - P. 39)

Draw the Cardigan
& A Line Skirt set
(see P. 116 - P. 117).

Add the eyes, eyebrows,
and mouth

Use brushed pen to finalize
the drawing.
Erase the containers

Colorize the character

Add highlights & shadows
(see P. 135)

KANAO

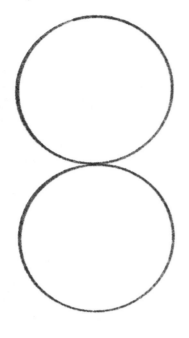

Draw 02 similar size circle

Divide the circles as the proportion described at P. 96

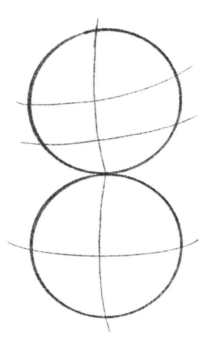

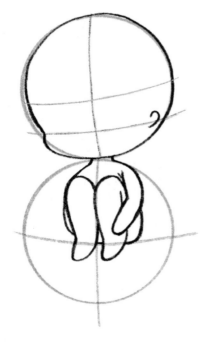

Draw the Sitting, Holding Knees pose (see P. 96 - P. 98)

Draw the Choppy Bangs &
Long Tying Twisted Side
(see P. 40 - P. 42)

Draw the Pajama set
(see P. 118 - P. 119).

Add the eyes, eyebrows,
and mouth

Erase the containers.
Use brushed pen to
finish sketching

Colorize the character

Add highlights & shadows
(see P. 135)

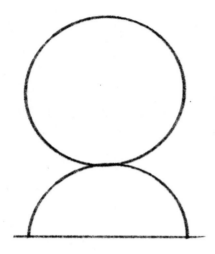

Draw the containers as this picture

Divide the circles as the proportion described at P. 99

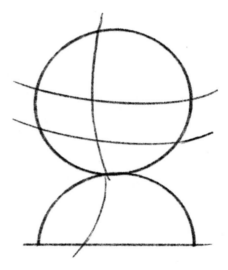

Draw the Sitting, Leaning Back pose (see P. 99 - P. 102)

Draw the Bob & Thick Bangs With Bun (see P. 43 - P. 44)

Draw the Turtleneck, Strap Skirt & Legging (see P. 120 - P. 121)

Add the eyes, eyebrows, and mouth

Erase the containers. Use brushed pen to finish sketching

Colorize the character

Add highlights & shadows (see P. 135)

SAIKI

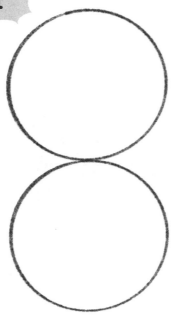

Draw 02 similar size circle

Divide the circles as the proportion described at P. 78

Draw the Wondering pose (see P. 78 - P. 80)

Draw the Cute Bob, Curly Hair (see P. 33 - P. 34)

Draw the Girl's Uniform set (see P. 109 - P. 110)

Add the eyes, eyebrows, and mouth

Erase the containers. Use brushed pen to finish sketching

Colorize the character

Add highlights & shadows (see P. 135)

ALICE

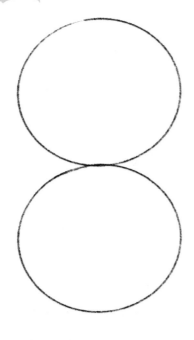

Draw 02 similar size circle

Divide the circles as the proportion described at P. 69

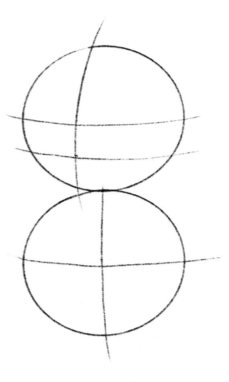

Draw the Stand, ¾ pose (see P. 69 - P. 71)

Draw the Shoulder Length Bob With Straight Bangs (see P. 35 - P. 36)

Draw the Wool Dress (see P. 111)

Add the eyes, eyebrows, and mouth

Erase the containers.
Use brushed pen to
finish sketching

Colorize the character

Add highlights & shadows
(see P. 135)

BOKU

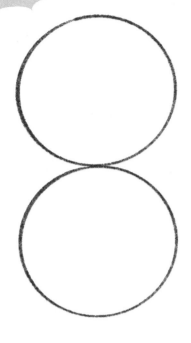

Draw 02 similar size circle

Divide the circles as the proportion described at P. 81

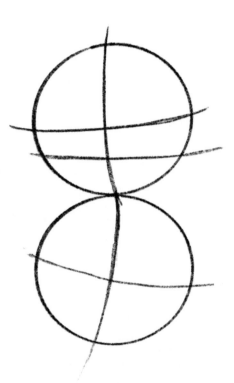

Draw the Greeting pose (see P. 81 - P. 83)

Draw the Cute Bob With Topknot hairstyle (see P. 31 - P. 32)

Draw the Winter Dress & Scarf (see P. 112 - P. 113)

Add the eyes, eyebrows, and mouth

Erase the containers. Use brushed pen to finish sketching

Colorize the character

Add highlights & shadows (see P. 135)

JUDY

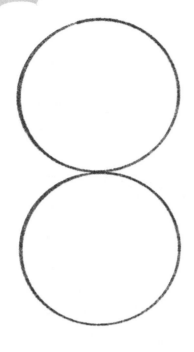

Draw 02 similar size circle

Divide the circles as the proportion described at P. 93

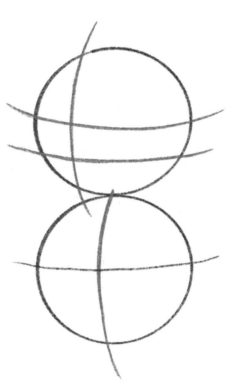

Draw the Walking pose (see P. 93 - P. 95)

Draw the Choppy Bangs With The Ponytail hairstyle (see P. 49 - P. 50)

Draw the Short Sleeve Shirt & Shorts (see P. 114 - P. 115)

Add the eyes, eyebrows, and mouth

Erase the containers.
Use brushed pen to
finish sketching

Colorize the character

Add highlights & shadows
(see P. 135)

DANNY

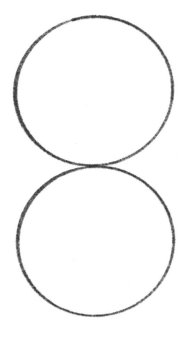

Draw 02 similar size circle

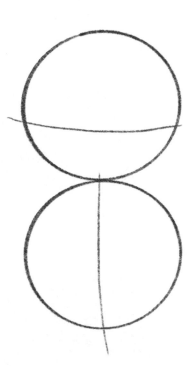

Divide the circles as the proportion described at P. 72

Draw the Stand, Side pose (see P. 72 - P. 74)

Draw the Long Messy Fringe,
Side View (see P. 57 - P. 58)

Draw the Hoodie and
Trousers
(see P. 133 - P. 134
and P. 128)

Add the eyes, eyebrows,
and mouth

Erase the containers.
Use brushed pen to
finish sketching

Colorize the character

Add highlights & shadows
(see P. 135)

JACKSON

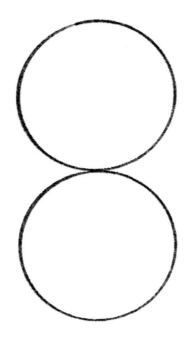

Draw 02 similar size circle

Divide the circles as the proportion described at P. 87

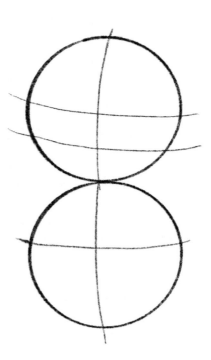

Draw the Serving pose (see P. 87 - P. 89)

Draw the Long Side Part Fringe (see P. 53 - P. 54)

Draw the Waistcoat & Shirt and Trousers (see P. 129 - P. 130 and P. 128)

Add the eyes, eyebrows, and mouth

Erase the containers. Use brushed pen to finish sketching

Colorize the character

Add highlights & shadows (see P. 135)

HUNTER

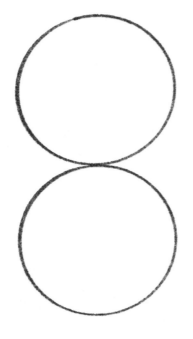

Draw 02 similar size circle

Divide the circles as the proportion described at P. 84

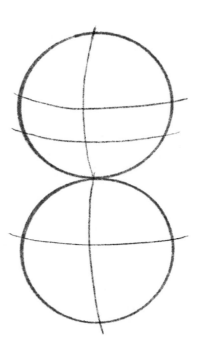

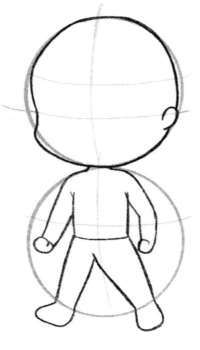

Draw the Determined pose (see P. 84 - P. 86)

Draw the Thick Brushed Up Fringe (see P. 55 - P. 56)

Draw the Short Sleeve T-Shirt and Trousers (see P. 127 and P. 128)

Add the eyes, eyebrows, and mouth

Erase the containers. Use brushed pen to finish sketching

Colorize the character

Add highlights & shadows (see P. 135)

YAIBA

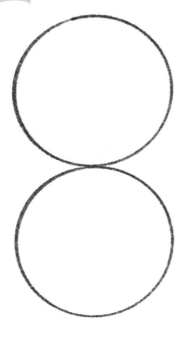

Draw 02 similar size circle

Divide the circles as the proportion described at P. 106

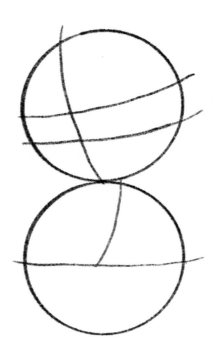

Draw the Sitting, Holding Chest pose
(see P. 106 - P. 108)

Draw the Long Messy Fringe (see P. 51 - P. 52)

Draw the Boy's Uniform and Trousers (see P. 131 - P. 132 and P. 128)

Add the eyes, eyebrows, and mouth

Erase the containers.
Use brushed pen to
finish sketching

Colorize the character

Add highlights & shadows
(see P. 135)

Printed in Great Britain
by Amazon

83584151R00106